CLEAN SLATE

9 Secrets To Getting a Job,
Even With A Felony!

MICHAEL LEWISTON

Copyright © 2012 Michael Lewiston

Published by Cantonfield Publishing

All rights reserved. No part of this book may be reproduced or transmitted in any form or by any means, electronic or mechanical, without permission in writing from the author.

ISBN: **1482054264**
ISBN-13: **978-1482054262**

DEDICATION

This book is dedicated to all those who believe in second chances, and starting fresh. To those who give second chances freely and a helping hand when it's desperately needed.

CONTENTS

Acknowledgments	i
Introduction	1
Secret #1	11
Secret #2	21
Secret #3	35
Secret #4	47
Secret #5	55
Secret #6	65
Secret #7	75
Secret #8	85
Secret #9	93
Extra Tip #1	101
Extra Tip #2	107
Final Thoughts	111
More Titles by Cantonfield Publishing	113

ACKNOWLEDGMENTS

Thank you to my beautiful wife for sicking by me through everything. It's been a crazy, long road but you have been there every step of the way. Thank you, thank you, thank you. I love you.

INTRODUCTION

Several years ago I was in prison. I was only down a couple of years but the label of "felon" made me generally unhireable to nearly every employer I talked to. Time and time again I would go in for an interview and fill out the application. There it was every time, the part that asks if you have ever committed a felony before, and I hated filling it out truthfully because I knew what that would lead to. No call, again. That's why I was so thankful that my friend, who owned a local home improvement company that sold windows and siding, took a chance on me and gave me a job in the marketing department.

I got lucky there. Not everyone does.

Basically I worked my butt off and got promoted a few times. I was making decent money and just so grateful that I even had a job. That's when it happened.

I walked into my work on a Thursday, it was the first of July, and my boss was helping one of my employees fill out an unemployment form on the internet. I worked in the home improvement industry, not known for its warm and caring nature, especially my boss, so this struck me as odd. My boss saw me as I walked in and ushered me into his office. "What's up?" I asked, a slow void building in the pit of my stomach. He looked at me briefly, then turned away, "I'm closing the company down, too much heat here. Moving the whole operation to Arizona if you want to come?"

I stood there in disbelief. Arizona? What? My family was here, my life was here, everything I knew and loved was in Washington State.

It was a done deal, he was moving. I politely declined his hasty offer to move across the country and he unceremoniously handed me a last paycheck. Not even a severance package. I drove home in a daze, a million questions pummeling my brain, and just as many concerns and fears jabbing at my emotions. What was I going to do now? First thing's first, I went and filled out my own unemployment form online, and entered the world of the unemployed. It was scary, nerve wracking, and I hated every minute of it.

Without going through the experience, no one can really know how it feels to have to look for a job. The pain and uncertainty of putting yourself out there, having to ask total strangers to take a chance on you, and the crushing defeat one feels when that dreaded rejection letter or email shows up. Even if you are completely qualified for the position, the lack of certainty can wear on you like nothing else. "Hunting" for a job simply isn't fun.

Millions of Americans know this feeling every year, and with the economy the way it is, millions more will continue to feel the bite of unemployment. Whether a student just starting out and looking for that first chance or a downsized senior manager, once in the unemployment pool we are all the same. There are few differences and we all share the same unfortunate circumstance, looking for the next paying job.

I was sure that I would find a new job soon, due to my background in marketing and employment counseling. My biggest hurdle was that I had that felony charge (non-violent, non-drug related) on my record. As you can imagine, that makes it a bit more difficult to secure a properly paying job. Within a week I had three offers, all at small to medium sized businesses, for positions that exceeded the salary of my previous job. I was ecstatic until I had to disclose what they would find on the background check, suddenly those same offers disappeared for various reasons.

This would be a common thread.

Every week I would apply to more jobs, and would get at least three offers every month, like clockwork. None of them panned out due to the background check, and honestly I became discouraged. You can only hear the same response so many times before you start to wonder if you will ever see the thing you want most, steady employment. But I chose not to give up, and instead devised a way to make my weaknesses strengths, catch a potential employer's eye right off the bat, and eventually I found a way to get hired despite a checkered past.

You need to know this, not to feel any sympathy for me, but to know that no matter what you're circumstance, I've walked in your shoes or been in worse situations. I took those hundreds of rejections and learned the true secrets to finding and staying employed in this economy. Distilling what works and what doesn't, I can now tell you with certainty that if you follow the secrets I lay out in this book, you can find a job more quickly and more easily than I did.

These secrets are simple yet powerful ways to get noticed and stand out from the crowd, but they not initially obvious to every job seeker. For example, in Secret #2 I'll show you one powerful way to make your resume stand out from everyone else, no matter what. And it will only take you a minute to do. If you learn these secrets, follow them as I lay them out, you will be happy, employed, and never have to worry about "job hunting" again.

It all starts with deciding what it is you really want to do.

SECRET #1: DECIDE WHAT YOU REALLY WANT!

Not understanding the power of this secret will tank your entire job search faster than anything else. If you have no idea what you want to find, your job hunt becomes unfocused and you move back in with your parents. I know from experience that being unemployed makes you feel that any job will do, like you have to search for anything and everything. But this doesn't have to be the case.

When I first began searching for a new job, I applied to several open marketing positions simply because I had a background in marketing. My focus was broad and I promoted myself as someone who could do all things marketing. While that was true because I have many different talents, it wasn't helpful to my search. By not drilling down and focusing on my major talents, I shot myself in the foot.

The responses to my resumes were less than impressive. Even the interviews that I managed to wrangle never went anywhere, mostly because the companies were looking for more specific skill sets, even if they didn't say that in the advertisement. Because I was so broad, they didn't know what to do with me. Hence, no job.

I knew that I couldn't keep trying the same old thing and expect different results. So I started listing all my specific skills.

At the home improvement company I had the opportunity to work on the website, writing some sales copy and doing some web design as well. I had to learn as I was going but it was great experience and something I enjoyed doing. Not only that, but I had samples of my work that I could show people and some numbers to show how effective the site and sales writing were in getting customers to buy windows. I also ran the phone room (yes, that means telemarketing) and the door to door canvassing program. I had management skills and knew how to work with people. These were great but I knew I needed more focus. I didn't know what until I spoke with a friend who ran a repo company.

Repossession Companies are not something you think about every day, unless you haven't paid your car note in a while. So when my friend Eric said his company was facing some stiff competition I was surprised. I never thought about repo guys having to compete with other companies, but apparently it's a big thing. Anyone with a truck can get into the repo business so Eric was having to fight for lower bid contracts against people willing to do the work for dirt cheap. Since he'd been in the business for over ten years, he wasn't willing to lower his prices down that far. He needed help. We started talking and I gave him some ideas, basically things that worked at my last job that might work for him as well. He was intrigued and offered me a job right then and there. Then came the moment of truth, I had to tell him about my criminal past.

Thankfully he was okay with that, having been in trouble himself many years ago, and he hired me on as his "marketing guy". Over the next year I did some great work for him, got paid on time and once again, was lucky enough to have a job. The experience taught me a few things. One, I wouldn't have been able to help Eric if I didn't know what my skills were. The ideas I gave him were about websites and sales techniques that I had learned at the home improvement job. If I hadn't sat down before and listed out all the things I knew how to do, then I couldn't have told him anything specifically helpful. The other thing I learned is that you have to pick an industry that you want to work in and that supports ex-offenders.

It's true that I kind of stumbled into the job. It was a very lucky break that I happened to talk to someone with a need, who knew me, and was forgiving about my past. But as I look back, there are lots of industries that have some grace for someone who's down on his luck. If I would have looked at those industries first, with a list of skills that I specifically brought to the table, then things would have been easier in my search. Industries like construction, home improvement, warehouse work, or even day labor work might be easy to see, but industries like repossession may not be obvious. Look for an industry that doesn't quite fit the traditional mold and start calling or emailing. Offer your services, maybe free of charge at first (if you are unemployed, what do you have to lose?), and let them know that if they like what you do, you expect a full time or even part time job later on.

So, know your skills and know the industries where you want to find work. Simple. Once you decided what you can offer, and where you want to work, it makes job searching a lot easier for you. It simplifies things so that you don't send out twenty resumes to places that may or may not get back to you. Instead you send out twenty resumes to places that need your skills and have a higher chance of bringing you on to work with them.

We will get into talking about friends and family later, but if you have supportive family and good friends, you need their help in finding a job. The one thing that makes it difficult for them to help you is when you aren't specific with them. If you just tell people "I just need a job" then they will be less likely to find a good job for you. But, if you tell them that you are good at a specific set of skills and you want to work in specific industries, then it makes it a lot easier for them to look for you.

This secret makes all the other ones possible. If you don't know what you want, or where you should look, it makes finding a job a lot harder, especially for someone with a record. You need to be smart about your job searching, work hard at finding your skills and the industries where you want to work, then use the rest of the tips to bring that job home.

If you do this tip right, your job search is half done.

Secret #2: Spice Up The Resume

I've tried sending out tons of differently styled resumes. Some had a little bit of color added, others were plain and generic, and then, when I was a little desperate, I tried some crazy stuff like bright, bold colors and illustrations. None of them worked as well as the resume I'm going to describe for you here. The trick is to be different from all the other resumes that people get, but not so different that the employer doesn't know what to make of it. You got to walk a fine line here, and if you follow my advice you can do just that.

The first thing you have to remember about a resume is that it's not for you, it's for the employer to find out if you can help them. Yes, you need a job, but the employer needs someone he can trust and that's more important to him than just giving you a job. You need to make your whole resume about how you are going to help the employer's business.

Some resumes use words like "I want to find a job in a field where I can grow…" Blah, Blah, Blah. That's all the employer hears, all the time, and it's not about him so he doesn't pay attention. You need to start using words like "I can help you…" and "I've done great things at my previous company, and I will do the same for you." That gets the employer's attention and makes him want to read more. You have to keep this in mind, that the employer is the only thing that matters, or else your resume won't get you anything except more unemployment.

A basic resume has some basic sections that most employers look for every time. The first is your name and contact information at the top. This should be easy to find and see, with your name in a large font at the top. Next, people usually put an "objective". I never add this my resumes because it's job seeker focused, not employer focused. Why would an employer care about your objectives?

Instead, I write a short but powerful statement about what I can do for the employer, something like "You are looking for a qualified [insert job title] to help you increase profits [or list another job duty] and my X years of experience will get that done for you." It's attention grabbing because it highlights your benefit to the employer, and it compels him to read farther.

Your contact information and "what you bring to the table" sections are necessary, you have to include them first, but the next section can vary a little. Either you can write up your employment history, or a list of your skills that will benefit the employer, or a combination of the two. I typically use both and try to make them complement each other.

I title the section below the statement of help something like "What I can do for you" and then list the skills I have in bullet point format along with the benefits to the employer. It's all about the employer. Say I'm talking about web design, but this could apply to customer service, framing, or even kitchen skills, I would say "3 years of web design experience that will help build your on line presence and increase your bottom line." Keep doing that with each skill, making a bullet point for each skill.

The next section should talk about your specific experiences, meaning jobs, but don't call them that. Label this section "Experience that will help you" and then list your jobs in chronological order. Under each job you want to talk about what you achieved. Some resumes simply list their job duties, but employers care more about what you achieved than what the last employer told you to do. This is where you can get pretty creative.

Say you worked at McDonald's, as a cashier. You weren't a cashier, you were a sales associate so that's what you put as your title. Sales associates are responsible for sales, right? So how much did sales increase when you were there? If you don't know the exact answer, give it your best guess. Did sales increase 10% or 30% while you were there? Put that down, just make sure come interview time you can explain how you came up with the number. The easiest way to fill in these sections below your jobs is to take your skills from the previous section and apply them to the jobs where you learned them. If one of your skills is customer service, then where did you learn customer service and what did you achieve at the job when you performed that skill well. This section fills in your story for the employer.

If you have a spotty work history I would suggest that you avoid listing achievements under each job, instead list your achievements and then your jobs. It's important to list your jobs in chronological order, the employer wants to see that even though he probably won't check up on you. Focus more on the skills that you bring to the table and hammer home the benefits of you working there.

The final section most employers look for is an education section. They want to see if you have any special degrees or certifications. If you didn't earn any degree when you were down, or before, then you might skip this section. However, if you took any classes that gave you special skills or certifications, then definitely list those if they apply to the job you want, meaning if they would be important to the employer.

Two final ideas about spicing up your resume are simple tricks that can give you amazing results. The first is adding a splash of color. Color instantly makes your resume stand out and get noticed so that the employer actually pays attention and reads the rest. Don't go crazy with color, just enough to stand out. I would suggest highlighting the contact information and each section heading. This will give your resume a nice, clean feel and break up the sections for easy reading. If you are making a resume in Microsoft Word then you can use the text background color for this. It works very well. But what color should you use?

Colors are funny, they can make you feel different things with just the slightest change of shade. Scientifically, blue and green are the most trustworthy and easy going colors. This is what you want to convey in your resume, that you are someone they can trust. Using blue in your headings psychologically changes the employer's mind for you, turning them from skeptical to enthusiastic about bringing you on board. Try it, you will see a huge improvement.

The last killer resume tip is to include a picture on the front. This might *seem* like a bad idea but if you are targeting your companies well, it should work better than most others at getting you the interview. Once I started doing this, my interviews automatically increased and every employer told me that they recognized me from my resume. They already had a face to put to the name.

Putting a picture of yourself on the resume makes the paper more human. Think about it, the employer goes through tons of resumes, all them boring and only words, then here is yours with color and picture of you smiling. Who do you think is going to get his attention? Some worlds of caution about what picture you choose. It has to be a picture where you are smiling and that makes you look good. Don't use a camera phone picture but find a friend or someone with a camera to take a picture of you. Look for a local landmark and wear your best clothes. Men should wear a suit and ladies should wear a pant suit or nice dress. The picture you take will only be a head shot, you want to make your face as visible as possible, so the employer may not see you nice clothes, but it will make you feel more confident. Make yourself look as professional as possible and you will make a great first impression.

Spicing up your resume isn't that hard, you just have to remember a few key points. Add headings that and sections that focus on the employer, not what you need. Talk about your skills and how they will benefit the employer. Add some good color to make your resume stand out. And finally insert a head shot picture of yourself smiling and looking very professional. If you do these things you will succeed at getting interviews.

Secret #3:

Get LinkedIn

The next couple secrets will be about the internet, which everyone has access to these days. If you don't have a computer in your home, or a friend or family member who will let you get online, there's always the library. As long as you have proof of your residence, you can get access to any library computer and complete any of these powerful secrets. The first secret is about using the power of the website LinkedIn.

LinkedIn allows professionals a safe place to look for work, hire employees, answer and ask questions that matter to their peers, and spy on the potential employers. I'm only slightly joking about the spying part.

You should use LinkedIn to establish yourself as a professional in your field. Add a resume, experience, education, skill lists, and ask people for recommendations. If you have a Blog, there's also a place to publish your Blog feed for visitors to see.

Overall, you can really benefit from LinkedIn through it's networking, groups, and it's question and answer engine. But first, you need to establish the all important profile.

- Establishing a Professional Profile -

First you need a professional looking photo, nothing that screams phone camera. If you took a picture for your resume I would recommend using that. Next get your resume and credentials in order. Then you need to find interesting things to say that you can do.

First things first. If you didn't take a picture for your resume, then you need one for the website. The photo you use for your profile must be a higher quality. Yes, camera phones can take pretty high resolution pictures, but everyone knows a photographer these days and most of them are using (or have access to) a better camera than your 5 megapixel phone camera. Call your friend up and ask if they will stage so shots for you as a favor or tell them they can add a watermark. Then offer them coffee, few can ignore the lure of fresh coffee.

Next, your resume has to be included somewhere on your profile. People want to see what you've done and achieved. Be certain that your LinkedIn resume doesn't differ from your resume that you send to employers.

The nice thing about your resume is that you can make it about whatever you want. The owners of LinkedIn aren't going to fact check you or make you provide proof of anything you say. This is NOT to say that you should fabricate anything, in fact that would destroy any chance of establishing your credibility. But, the open nature of the system allows you to have the freedom to create titles, job descriptions, or new skills.

Especially if you work for yourself, you are bound to pick up some alternative skill sets that might not be appreciated widely in the corporate world. If your focus is to get a corporate job then that's the audience you need to focus on. A small business, then focus on that. Then it's time to start telling stories about your previous work.

Use this section to repeat your resume in an online form. You can add it word for word or you can add some more details. It's up to you. Make sure that you make it clear that you are looking for a new job, in a specific industry. That way anyone interested in your profile will know what you want.

- Posting Updates That Matter -

LinkedIn has an update feature that looks a lot like the update feature in Facebook. The difference is in the audiences.

Updates on LinkedIn should be more substantial than Facebook or even Twitter posts. In fact, you would do well to only post links to websites that contain useful or helpful information. Personal status updates are best saved for the other sites.

You can use the update feature to push your messages or you can use it to share useful information and stories. Can you guess by now which one I advocate?

Use the updates feature to share articles on websites that have piqued your interest. Employer can go to your profile and see what your last posts have been. That means they will get an idea what you are thinking at any given moment. That can be very powerful for your credibility. If you say you are an expert or skilled in a certain area, and you are posting links for those areas, the employer is more likely to believe that you have those skills.

- Groups and Discussion -

Groups are a powerful feature within any social network. They combine the ease of use and personality of a modern website with the power of forums and discussion groups. You can find a groups section fairly easily, it's finding the group that you want to invest in that's the hard part.

Groups on LinkedIn allow you the opportunity to connect with people in your field, talk directly to potential employers, and show off your experience and expertise. They are not a place to promote your job search directly. Here more than any other place on the site, other people don't put up with that behavior. That doesn't mean you can't get a little creative.

It's easy if you look for the opportunities available to you. The main concern on the groups pages is to connect with other people by lending them your expertise. Groups make it easy by clarifying what everyone there is interested in. If you join a group and look for ways to help others with your expertise, then you get noticed as someone that helps. Half the people on LinkedIn are employers in one way or another so it's likely that one of the people you help in your group will be able to hire you.

Take advantage of the groups feature, they work.

- Questions and Answers -

Like groups in the sense that you are lending a hand, is the Answers section. In this area of LinkedIn, people ask questions and any member of the site can answer them. It is open to everyone.

If you have a wide breadth of information, but no deep expertise, this can help in two ways. First, it can give you the opportunity to answer generally without having to get into too much detail, as can happen in the group's question and answer sessions.

It can also be a chance for you to ask some questions outside of your field and connect with those that can demonstrate their authority.

Plus, if you're struggling for blog post ideas, interacting with people, answering questions, are all great ways to generate ideas. Plus you never know who you are helping and how that can turn into a job down the road.

If you are using LinkedIn, just keep these things in mind: fill out your profile in full, post cool websites that relate to your skills, join relevant groups and contribute, and answer questions. Do these things consistently and you will see some real success with LinkedIn.

Secret #4: Tell Facebook Your Troubles

Everyone I know these days has a Facebook account. It's everywhere and unless you have restrictions on your internet usage, you should have one too. Not only can it be a great way to connect with family and friends, but you can also easily enlist their help with your job search. For this to work you need to set up an account and friend a bunch of people that you know. Like I said, family and real life friends are a good place to start. If you already have a Facebook account with a lot of friends then you are already off to a good start.

So then how do you get your friends on Facebook to help you?

You could just put up a status update that says, "Hey, I need a job. Anyone know of any?" but if you learned the first secret, you know that this is not the most effective way to ask for help.

You could try to post a status update about the skills you have to offer and the industries you are looking to work in. But this might be kind of boring for people to read, not that they don't care about you, but you have to think of them as well. Just like with the employers, you have to keep in mind who you are talking to. What's in it for the person reading your post? Sure they get to help you out and feel good about making a difference, but can't you give them something else?

Here are two great ideas for sharing your job search on Facebook.

The first is to use pictures. Status updates that are all words are not as interesting as pictures. People sometimes read all word updates but it's so much easier to just look at a picture and see what is going on. Plus, pictures can tell what's happening a lot easier and faster than just words.

Here's what you can do, take a picture of yourself frowning into a camera with a sign that says "Need To Work". Make sure the frown is really big so that people will think it looks funny or cheesy. If you make people laugh then they will be more likely to help you. Then you can add your skills and industries in the words section of the update.

An even better idea would be to show yourself doing the job that you are looking for.

If you want to get a construction job, take a picture of you doing some work with a hammer and smiling. Then in the words section you write something like "Hey Everyone, been trying to get a job and it's pretty tough out there. Anyone who knows me knows that I work hard. But I need your help with something. I really good at [insert skills] and I'm trying to work with a business in [insert industry]. If you could share this pic or let me know if you know anyone who might be hiring, that would be a big help." Your words will differ obviously.

The point is that they will see you picture, then read your question. The picture makes everyone many times more likely to read what you wrote. And they will be more likely to help you since you gave them something, a simple picture.

I know it doesn't sound like much, but that picture could mean a lot to the friend seeing it. It makes your asking for help more real and human. Plus, if it's funny, people will scramble to share it. People like sharing things that are funny because it makes them look funny too. But you don't have to do just one picture, what if you did a series of pictures with you around the house or out and about doing the things that you want to do for a job.

You could post one picture a week and let people know how your job search is going, maybe even telling a few funny stories along the way. One thing to keep in mind, *this is not a pity party*. The second you start to mope and get negative, people will stop helping you. Stay positive and just try to share what's happening in your life, and you should get a good response from your friends on Facebook.

If you just think of Facebook as a way to show people that you are honestly hoping to work and you can say it in a fun way, then you should see a lot of success with this. Just think, how many other people don't have jobs and are doing something like this? Not many, or any, which means you will stand out. So get on Facebook if you are not already there, start taking some pictures, and let your friends online know your story.

Secret #5: Using Email to Extend Your Search

This secret can be one of the most powerful things you can do, but also one of the scariest. This is similar to the Facebook secret but much more personal because you will be sending an email to individuals, not just putting something out there for all to see. The idea is to let your friends and family know in a very personal way, that you need their help and exactly how they can help you.

I know that this is scary to think about. Emailing your friends and family directly, asking for help? Are you crazy? Not at all. It is a lot more personal and direct than just throwing up a status update on Facebook, so the fear of rejection and upsetting someone is high. That's okay. If they care about you and you make your email heartfelt, then you won't upset them. You will only let them know you need help.

The other thing you might not like about writing emails to your friends and family, is that it seems too sales-like. You might read this and think to yourself that it feels like you are going to try to sell your family and friends into helping you. You do have to do that, in a way, but not a bad way. You have to convince them that you are worth helping and that it will be very easy to do that.

When you write your emails, don't send a bunch all at once. Address them individually to each person you want to send to and say their name at the top of the email. Let them know what's been going on in your job search, in a positive way, and that you still haven't found a place to work. If you are positive about the rest of the experience, just saying that you still haven't found a job is more than enough to let them know you need help.

Then you let them know your skills and what industries you are looking at. Go over all this very briefly and don't get into too much detail. The less they have to remember, the better. This might seem counter to what feels right, but if you tell them too much then they will get confused. Instead, you want to give them bare details of your abilities, where you want to apply those abilities, and most importantly, how this person can help you.

You might be thinking, how can they help me? It can be in many ways, but some of it depends on who you are emailing. Some of your friends and family might have special contacts or information that might help you in your search. That's why you don't send out a huge email addressed to everyone all at once, you want to maximize the personal touch. Just ask them if they know of anyone or anything open in the industries you talked about. If not, no big deal. You had to try. Then let them know there is one way they can help.

Ask them to email your resume out to their friends and family.

This move takes huge balls, because you are asking someone to send out your information cold to people in their address books. If you do this right, it might be the most effective thing you do in your job search, and land you a new job within a week or two. Here's what you do.

After you explain your situation, your skills, desired industry, and ask them about their inside connections, let them know that if they can't help with connections, could they at least do a little something for you that could make a big difference? Tell them that the best way they could help, unless they know of a job, is to tell their friends about you.

Now, you don't just ask them to tell friends about you. First you attach a resume to the email in PDF form. If you don't have a program (like Open Office) that will convert your resume to a PDF file, just use the format you have. Point is to attach a resume, as well as copy and paste the text in the body of the email at the very bottom. Then you write an email for your friend or family member to send to their contact list. They can just attach you resume and copy and paste the email you wrote for them. You do the work for them and make it easy, that's the only way this will happen.

The email that you write for your friend or family member to send should say something similar to what you just wrote. Begin with something like "Hey, I know this is out of the blue but my friend needs a favor and I've never been one to turn down someone when they need help. [Name] is looking for a job in the [name of industry] and he's really talented, specializing in [skills]. If you know of anyone looking to hire someone in this industry, let him know. His email is [email]. Also, his resume is attached if you want to look it over. If you don't know of anything, would you mind sending this email out to your email contacts like I did. He would really appreciate it and you would be doing a good thing. Thanks for reading and I really hope you can help out."

Use the text above as a sample but write something close to that. If you do this right, then your friend will feel comfortable sending out the email, and then his or her friends will resend it to their friends, who might send it to their friends. Do you see how powerful this is?

Say you only have 20 friends and family that you send this email with your resume to. Then each of those 20 people send it to thirty people, that makes 600 extra people, outside your friends and family, who have seen your resume and skills. What if those 600 people send it to their friends? Say those 600 only send it to 20 people each, that's 12,000 people! Do you see how amazing this could be for you? Not only will this secret get your resume seen, but it also shows initiative. Employers like to see that and especially if you have a criminal background, you need every employer thinking of you as someone they can rely on, not as a former criminal.

This secret is not easy to pull off, but if you have the guts to get it done, and you are smart about how you write your email, then this could be the most powerful tool in your job seeking career.

Secret #6: Develop Professional Interview Techniques

Getting the job is not all about sending out resumes and making contacts with employers. You have to get interviews and do well in them if you want to get hired. The whole reason you send out resumes is to get the interview, so if the interview is the goal, then you should learn some ways to be extra effective and make your interview the best one it can be.

Most people are not that good at interviews. Either they get nervous or they aren't prepared, they go into the interview thinking they will be fine and they totally blow it. You can avoid this by following a few tips that end up getting you the job you want.

The first thing to remember in any interview situation is that you have to keep the employer in mind at all times. You have to think to yourself, what would they want from an ideal employee? The very basic thing you can do right out the gate, is show up to the interview a little early with a smile on your face.

Few things make a better impression on a future boss than showing up before you are "supposed to be there". Take the time of the interview and aim to be there 10-15 minutes earlier than that. Showing up early is a sure fire way to show your potential boss that you respect him and his time. Never forget that small point and you will do just fine. Come early and come prepared.

Another good tip to remember relates to what you wear. When it comes to dressing, there's lots of advice out there and most it will help, but not all of it at once. There's just too much to take in and it probably won't help you in the end. Here's a simple, scientifically proven way to stand out, dress 10% better than you think your boss will be dressed.

If you are going to an interview for a construction job, don't dress in a suit, but your boss probably won't be wearing jeans with holes in them either. This requires some guessing but it's worth the effort. You only have to dress a little better and you'll be better liked. If you dress too well, then the employer may think you are trying to be better than them. If you dress down, the employer may think you just don't care about the job and won't hire you for that. It's a fine line, but if you aim for 10% better, you will usually hit your mark. A good rule to keep in mind is to try and dress better than you do normally.

Another thing potential employees do at interviews that sinks their chances, is not being confident. This isn't saying you should be cocky or full of yourself, but confident that you are worth hiring and deserve the job. This is especially hard for honest ex-offenders who need a job but have been told "No" so many times that they start to believe that they are not worth the employer's time. You are and you have to believe that. You are good and you deserve a chance to show what you can do. However, don't walk through the door with a bunch of swagger, hoping to impress the boss with your ability to talk a good game. It probably won't work, in fact studies have shown it doesn't. The boss is the boss and you are there to work for him. That doesn't make you any less but you need to keep it in mind.

Honest and sincere confidence, the kind that stems from self-worth and knowing your value, is the best way to get remembered. Employers are interviewing all the time, sometimes seeing hundreds of people a day. Who are they going to remember? The guy who mumbled and didn't say much, or the man who said in clear tones, 'Yes Sir' and spoke his mind, knew his skills and exactly why he was a good fit for the job. When you go into any interview, be confident that the employer saw something he liked and wants to see more. Show it to him and the job should be yours.

A final tip for giving a great interview is to do some research. Sometimes it helps to think of this as you interviewing the boss at the same time he's interviewing you, deciding whether or not you want him for an employer. Even if you are hard up for a job, you need to walk into the interview willing to walk away if the situation isn't right. Even if that is not your intention, the boss needs to get the impression that this is your intention. Again, don't be too brash or arrogant about it, but let them know you want to know more about them. You can signal all this by asking good questions about the boss and the company. Ask them good, probing questions and you should win the boss's respect and sail through the end of the interview.

Your interview is the next step in getting hired, so don't leave it to the last moment. You can have a great resume, do some fine networking, but if you are not very good at interviewing you will have a very hard time landing that job. Practice your interview skills, learn the tips in this section, and you should be on your way to having your next great interview and soon, a job.

Secret #7:

Do Something With Your Time

Two men went into interviews at a local warehouse for a forklift driver position. They weren't the only guys going for this job, so they were a little nervous about their chances. Both of them had good resumes, interviewed well, smiled, and dressed right. But one got the job while the other didn't even get a call back. Why? Because the one who got the job was already doing something else with his time.

There's an old saying that it's easier to find a job when you have a job than when you don't have one. That's true, because employers like to hire people that are already employed, makes them less risky. You don't have that going for you, but you can do the next best thing. You can stay busy and do some interesting things with your life. The guy applying for the job that didn't get hired and the guy who did were asked the same question; What do you like to do in your spare time? If there is a gap in your recent employment history, the employer will almost always ask this.

What's your answer?

The typical answers of reading and watching TV won't do anymore, employers expect more from their employees. In fact, the guy who didn't get the warehouse job talked about playing lots of video games. He said it as a joke, kind of, but the employer didn't think it was funny.

If you are out of work for any amount of time, and you choose to spend that time playing video games or just watching a lot of TV, that will signal to the employer that you don't have good priorities. The guy who did get hired at the warehouse started his answer by saying that he had some time on his hands recently and then talked about the new cooking dishes he was working on. This led to the employer asking about the dish which led to a conversation about cooking in general. The man came across as interesting and proactive, two things that employers absolutely love.

Instead of using your extra time to entertain yourself, you need to give yourself every advantage, especially when you have a record. Every employer is going to look at your with a certain caution from now on, and you have to do everything in your power to make them see you differently. So instead of watching more TV or playing Call of Duty, learn a skill. Write a book. Start a blog. Learn how to build websites. Paint. Cook. Find a hobby or a craft. Get an unpaid internship at an office. Just do something with your time more interesting than entertaining yourself.

If you are reading this while you are inside, pay special attention. Everyone does their time in their own way, but if you care about increasing your chances of getting a job, you should try to improve yourself. You could sit in the TV room all day, or read every Sci-Fi novel in the library, but you could also learn a new skill or start a new hobby. The possibilities are endless when you stop limiting yourself.

The resources are out there for you to learn. Everything you could want to know about now is on the internet and there are probably thousands of websites geared toward teaching the skill that you want to acquire. Even if you are going for a manual labor job, having extra skills that the employer could possibly use in the future is a great thing to have and makes you more desirable. And more desirable means you get the job.

So what if you don't have any interests? What if your interests are not exactly "business related" and you don't think any employer would be interested?

I have a friend who loves to sing and rap. On the surface these don't look like things that employers would like to hear about, and taken by themselves that would probably be correct. But what if you started uploading these songs to the internet? That means you have to put up quality videos or sound files, so you have to learn a little about audio engineering. What if you started to learn about websites and promotion because you were marketing your videos? Now you have internet experience, video and sound editing, as well as marketing experience. Even companies that don't necessarily use those kinds of services can respect that, but what if you could help them in your own unique way?

Say you had all these skills, what's stopping you from offering to help them produce a short video that will appeal to a certain demographic, for free? Why not? It's a win, win situation. You get the experience and something to show for your work, and they get a quality production. Make sure you tell them that if they don't like it they don't have to use it, no problem. Do that and you have clinched the deal and probably got yourself a job.

No matter who you are, or what you want to do, there is a way to improve yourself. The cooking example I gave earlier was actually something that happened to a friend of mine a couple of years ago. He was laid off from his job and looking for work. We was always interested in Indian food so he decided to get some books from the library and start to learn. He actually got pretty good at making that type of food, so when the time came for him to answer what he did with his time, there was no hesitation. Now, he was applying for a job with as a forklift driver, so cooking wasn't part of the employment description, but it gave the employer the impression that this was someone that did things. He got the job and has been a valued employee ever since.

So, when you are not looking for a job, try to do something incredible and interesting with your time. Find something to do worth talking about and that will help your life down the road. Nothing says loser like not growing as a person and employers don't hire losers. Find what you want to do and start small. Don't expect to be an expert right away and you should get pretty good at whatever it is you choose to do.

Secret #8:

Be Honest But Not Always Right Away

When you are trying to get a job, honesty really is the best policy, but it doesn't mean you have to tell the employer everything right away. I see this as one of the biggest things that ex-offenders, both with felonies and misdemeanors, struggle with; how much to tell and when to tell it. The secret is in the when, because you have to tell them everything.

Back when I was laid off, I had to find a job while I was on parole. If you think it's hard to find work just because of your record, it's even harder to find it when your PO has to call the work to make sure you are working there and that they know you are an ex-con. There's no getting around that, the employer had to know and I had to tell. Every interview was stressful because I knew that somewhere I had to disclose that I was on parole. I would always see the employer's face drop, because they liked me, but this was too much. Eventually I found a job despite this but I know how much it sucks.

Here's what I learned to be the key. Don't say anything unless asked, not until you know that they are serious about hiring you. Telling people proactively that you are a felon is admirable but it will quickly end your chances of being hired if you do it too early in the process. Better for both you and the employer if you wait to disclose that little bit of information until later, this goes double for those on probation and parole. If it's going to take multiple interviews to get the job, wait until the very last moment to say anything.

One thing you must never do is write anything that's not true on your application, that's actually illegal. It can be very tempting to skip that section, answer no, and try to avoid taking responsibility but the consequences of getting caught are higher than the truth. What I found, funny enough, is that a lot of employers don't even look at that section if you have your other ducks in a row. In fact, eight out of ten times they were surprised when I told them about the parole issue, even though I clearly stated my crime on the resume. Eventually this process paid off for me, but it would have been worthless without my carefully crafted story.

When you sit down with your potential employer, you need to have something ready to say when they ask you about your past.

Creating a well thought out story is the simplest way to get over this hurdle. Whatever you do, do not just wing it. Something you come up with on the spot will never be as good as a well prepared story that you make beforehand and memorize. Here's why this works; everyone loves a good story. By good I mean one that follows certain story rules that we are all familiar with – a guy, who wants something and must overcome hardship to get it with a satisfying ending. If you tell a story like this then you will blow the employer away with your struggle to get where you are now, how far you have come, and how ready you are to make different choices and turn your story around.

I recommend you use the following as a sample to go off of, but of course your story will be different:

You got into trouble in the past because of poor choices, those are done with now, you have done these things to give back to the community, you are ready and able to work, you'll do a better job because you have something to prove to them.

Once you tell your story, all the rest should make sense for a goodhearted employer. As long as you are honest about your past, most people have compassion with this and they will tell you how good it is that you have made other choices. They might not hire you but it takes the sting out of telling people about your past mistakes and bad situations. However, if you learn the other secrets and do everything right, you should have a new job waiting for you and an employer glad to have you on board. There's just one more thing you might want to think about doing and it will be the icing on the cake, the one secret that might get you the most mileage at the end of a long interview. We'll discuss that next.

Secret #9: Give Something Back in Your Spare Time

In addition to improving yourself, what else is there to do? What another episode of your favorite TV show? Play another game?

Why not do some charity work?

If you want to prove to an employer that you have changed, this might be the most visible way you can show you are making different actions. Improving yourself is one thing, but showing that you are actively trying to improve other people is another matter entirely.

Here's why this works. Most crimes are selfish ones, where you were trying to get something for yourself or make yourself feel good. Whether or not that was the case, that's what people think. That's also why they are worried about hiring an ex-offender because they are worried that you will put your interests above theirs, basically that you might lie, or steal, or take advantage of their trust. So how do you show the employer that you are not the guy you used to be? By giving back to your local community in some meaningful way.

Nothing makes you look like you have reformed more completely than giving your time, on a regular basis, to other people in need. A consistent pattern of helping others makes you more desirable than other candidates because it means you don't always just think about yourself, you want to give to others and help people. This is a rare and wanted trait in most companies. If you can show this then you have an automatic leg up on your competition of a job.

I would recommend giving as much free time as you can spare, at least once a week, to a local charity. It doesn't matter what the charity is, all that matters is that you are giving regularly. Regular is key. You have to commit to a schedule and keep it or else it says something negative about you. This isn't easy, but the benefits are incredible. As you are working, get to know the supervisor and carefully explain your situation. Go back to the first secret and tell them what your skills are, what industry you are looking for work in, and then how you got to where you are. Most people that work in charity and non-profits have heard many stories, but they don't often get to hear about successes. You are a success story so they will be happy to help down the road if you are consistent and true to your word.

That's the key, you have to be true to your word and consistent, then this relationship with the supervisor can bring two benefits. One, they would be a great reference for any employer. More than likely your employer will want to check on you, make sure what you have told him is true. How great would it be if he called the charity where you have donated your time and there was this supervisor who gave you a glowing recommendation! That right there is worth every minute that you donate to your charity, but there's one more benefit. Possible networking. If you tell your supervisor who you are and what you want to do, then you prove that you are a consistent and good worker, if he or she hears about something along those lines that comes up, don't you think they would be more likely to recommend you for that job?

Lots of people get jobs this way, in fact getting a job through personal connections is the best way to get a job. If your supervisor at the charity hears about a job and recommends you, that holds a lot more weight to the employer than just sending in a resume. None of this is to say that you should work at a charity just to get these benefits, but they do help. Even if you start out at the charity or non-profit just to help your job search, if you are consistent in going, you will be changed as well.

One of the best things about charity work is that it actually makes you happier and a better person. There have been a lot of studies about this, and each one shows that the more we give, the happier we become. If you begin to give to others, you will not only become a better person but others will want to give to you. So steal yourself, start giving to charities regularly, help others on a regular basis, and make a good contact in the charity that you are helping. That way you will be set, not only in your job but also a better person in your life.

Extra Tip #1: Men Will Be More Likely To Hire You

This isn't intended to be sexist or mean, it's just biology and repeated experience. Men in general have a higher tolerance for what they think might be risky, so they are more likely to hire someone with a checkered background than a woman would be. This applies for both men and women being hired. Just because you are a female, don't believe that another woman is more likely to hire you, that's not the case. A female employer is going to be making a more harsh judgment on you than a male one. That's because she is designed to protect her young from danger, a natural instinct, and once you tell her that you have a criminal past, you are a danger. A male employer is able to look at the situation more objectively and judge you on your merits.

Think of it this way, if you accidentally hit a child with your car door in the parking lot of the supermarket, would you rather deal with the Mom or the Dad? In my experience the Father is likely to look at the situation less emotionally and more rationally while the Mother reacts to the situation and starts screaming. Again, this is not a judgment, just an observation.

So should you avoid female employers? Not necessarily, but avoid them if you can. If you walk into a situation where you are being interviewed by a woman and she will be your boss, don't let that discourage you. Instead, keep her biology in mind and turn her fear of you into a desire to protect you. Get to know her and let her get to know you. It's not easy to do but if you can make her think of you as one of her own then you have successfully turned the tables and beat the odds.

Extra Tip #2: Make Friends with your Parole or Probation Officer

If you read secret number 9, then you know the power of having a voice on your side recommending you for the position or telling the employer how great you are. Would your PO say the same? If you are probation or parole you are required to disclose your incarceration status, which means your PO is going to call and check on your place of employment. If you don't tell your employer about your felony or criminal background when you are hired, then they will certainly find out then! Instead, honesty is the best policy and having your PO on your side can be a great help in getting a job.

So what are they going to say about you? Have you stayed out of trouble? Have you been a role model for others and without any question should be released from custody soon? I recently landed my current job as an advertising copywriter because of my PO's recommendation. I included her as one of my references and when I disclosed my felony charge, I told the employer to call and get an unbiased opinion of my character and habits. I've been good the whole time I was on paper so my PO gave a great recommendation. The boss was able to trust me and I got the job. Make friends with your PO if possible, let them know who you are and what you want. Once they think of you as a person things will go a lot more smoothly for you.

Final Thoughts

You are not your past. It's important to remember that as you start looking for work. So many times you will want to give up or start thinking it's hopeless, but it's not. You will succeed and I've just given you nine secrets to help you get ahead. You have the tools to get yourself ready and find a job today. If you have to, read this book again and again, so that you understand how to accomplish each tip. Work hard at this, and you will find yourself with a job in no time.

ENJOY MORE TITLES FROM CANTONFIELD PUBLISHING

Go Write Now! - How to free yourself from the tyranny of traditional publishing and become a successful publishing author by Josh Kilen

The Greatest Thoughts Never Heard by Brant W. Maxwell

How to Win the Lottery by Noah Canfield

And more coming soon, just go to cantonfield.com to check out the latest titles.

Made in the USA
Columbia, SC
02 May 2024